A Fish Called

MW01228435

Story by Jackie Tidey
Photography by Lindsay Edwards

SULLIVAN ELEMENTARY SCHOOL
6016 - 152 STREET
SURREY, B.C.
V3S 3K6
36021

PET
SHOP
←

2

Ramon and Mum

went into a pet shop.

"Can I have a pet, please, Mum?"

said Ramon.

"It will have to be a small one,"

said Mum.

"Our house is not very big."

"This puppy is small,"
said Ramon.

"It is now," said Mum.
"But this puppy
will grow into a big dog."

"Look at this little kitten,"
said Ramon.
"Kittens don't grow very big."

"You have to play with kittens,
Ramon," said Mum.
"I will be at work all day
and you will be at school."

"Rabbits don't grow very big, and you don't have to play with them all the time," said Ramon.

"Rabbits have to stay outside in a cage," laughed Mum.

Ramon looked at the fish
swimming around in the tanks.

He saw a little black fish
with white stripes.

He saw fat fish
with long wavy tails.

SULLIVAN ELEMENTARY SCHOOL
6016 - 152 STREET
SURREY, B.C.
V3S 3K6

11

Then Ramon saw a funny little fish hiding under some plants.

The little fish swam out of the plants.

"Mum," said Ramon.
"Come here and look at this funny little fish with big eyes."

"Can I have this little fish for a pet?" said Ramon.

"Yes," smiled Mum.
"A fish will make a good pet."

"Thanks, Mum," said Ramon.

"I am going to call you Goggles,"
said Ramon.
"You are the best fish in the shop."